P9-AQG-172

What Does GREEN Mean?

Barbara L. Webb

ROURKE PUBLISHING

www.rourkepublishing.com

© 2012 Rourke Publishing LLC

www.rourkepublishing.com

PHOTO CREDITS: Cover: © Shawn Gearhart, SalmonX; Title Page: © Amber Antozak; Page 4: © Alina Solovyova-Vincent; Page 5: © Atid Kiattisaksiri; Page 6: © Morgan Lane Studios; Page 7: © Nickilford; Page 9: © René Mansi, Murat Giray Kaya, Jamie McCarthy; Page 10: © Pauline S. Mills; Page 11: © Sandy Jones; Page 12: © Aydin Mutlu; Page 13: © James McQuillan; Page 14: © Kenryk Sadura; Page 15: © Msats, Darlene Sanguenza; Page 17: © Alexandr Mitiuc, Ping Han, Murat Giray Kaya; Page 19: © Carmen Martínez Banús, Catherine Yeulet, Aldo Murillo; Page 20, 21: © Rosemarie Gearhart;

Edited by Meg Greve

Cover and Interior design by Tara Raymo

Library of Congress Cataloging-in-Publication Data

Webb, Barbara L.
  What Does Green Mean? / Barbara L. Webb.
    p. cm. -- (Green Earth Science Discovery Library)
  Includes bibliographical references and index.
  ISBN 978-1-61741-771-9 (hard cover) (alk. paper)
  ISBN 978-1-61741-973-7 (soft cover)
  Library of Congress Control Number: 2011924817

Rourke Publishing
Printed in the United States of America, North Mankato, Minnesota
060711
060711CL

ROURKE PUBLISHING

www.rourkepublishing.com - rourke@rourkepublishing.com
Post Office Box 643328 Vero Beach, Florida 32964

Table of Contents

What Does Green Mean?

Everyone talks about living green, but what does green mean?

Living green means making big and small choices that are gentle on the Earth.

The color green reminds us of a healthy
Earth filled with growing and living things.

Do you like the idea of a healthy Earth?
Then let's learn how to live green!

Eco-friendly Choices

Green choices are **eco-friendly** and do not harm the Earth's **environment**.

We make eco-friendly choices when we use less of things, such as paper, fuel, and electricity.

When we use less, we make less trash, pollute less, and take fewer resources from the Earth.

We make eco-friendly choices when we make things out of materials that the Earth can **absorb**.

Most foam packing material does not break down in a landfill. Scientists are working on growing eco-friendly packing material out of mushroom roots!

Cardboard packaging can be **recycled**,
but most plastic packaging sits in a **landfill**
for years without breaking down. Which is
the eco-friendly choice to buy?

Buying food from **organic** or **sustainable** farms is an eco-friendly choice. These kinds of farms only use plant food and bug sprays that the Earth can absorb.

The ladybug beetle eats insects that damage crops so organic farmers do not need to use poisonous bug sprays.

Even your red, blue, and orange fruits and vegetables can be green!

Carbon Footprints

Have you checked the size of your **carbon footprint** lately? Don't look down at your feet! A carbon footprint measures the harmful **greenhouse gases** a person, building, or business makes.

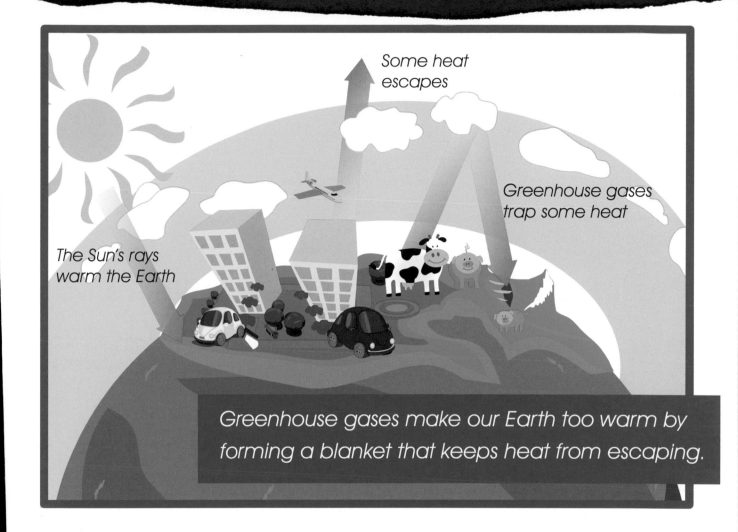

The fuel in our cars makes a greenhouse gas. The cows and pigs we farm for meat make greenhouse gases with their waste.

Your carbon footprint is larger if you drive to school rather than walk. Your carbon footprint is larger if you eat a lot of meat rather than a little.

What's Your Carbon Footprint?

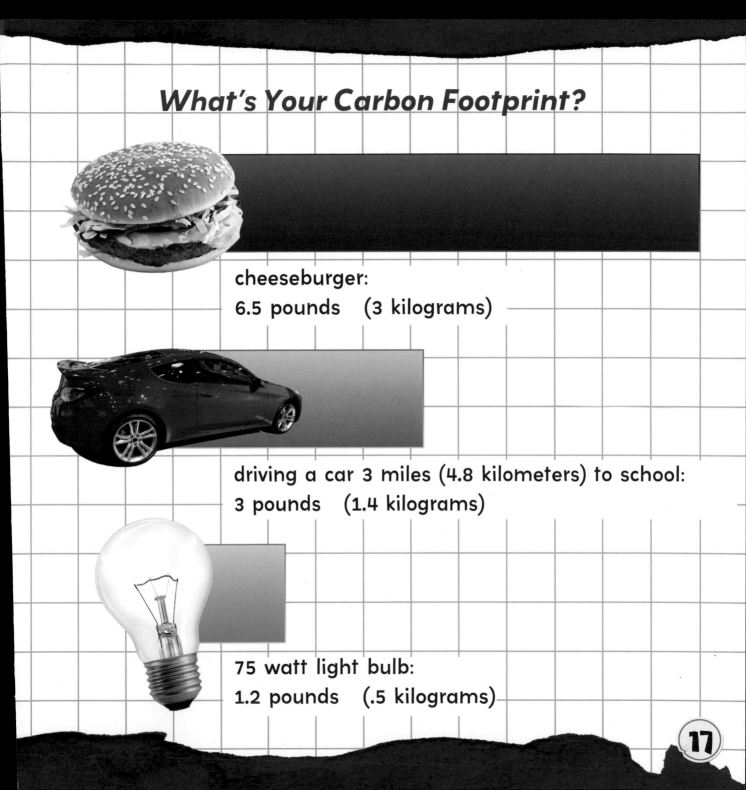

cheeseburger:
6.5 pounds   (3 kilograms)

driving a car 3 miles (4.8 kilometers) to school:
3 pounds   (1.4 kilograms)

75 watt light bulb:
1.2 pounds   (.5 kilograms)

You Can Live Green!

What kinds of green choices can you make? Recycling? Walking? Eating more fruits and vegetables?

Make eco-friendly choices and watch your carbon footprint shrink!

Recycling 7 million tons (6 million metric tons) of metal is like taking 4.5 million cars off the road for a year!

Be proud of yourself
for living green!

Try This

For three days, write down all the things you and your family do that add to your carbon footprint, such as:

Activity	Day 1	Day 2	Day 3
Number of miles you drive			
Number of minutes in the shower			
Number of times you throw something away instead of recycling			
Number of times you eat meat			
Number of pages you print on a printer			
Number of loads of laundry			

When the three days are done, look at your list and talk with your family about how to make these numbers smaller and shrink your carbon footprint.

Glossary

absorb (ab-ZORB): to soak up

carbon footprint (KAR-buhn FUT-print): the amount of greenhouse gases someone or something puts into the environment

eco-friendly (EE-koh-FREND-lee): not harmful to the Earth's environment

environment (en-VYE-ruhn-muhnt): all the natural parts of the Earth like water, air, and plants

greenhouse gases (GREEN-houss GASS-iz): gases such as carbon dioxide and methane that hold heat next to the Earth

landfill (LAND-fil): a place where trash is buried

organic (or-GAN-ic): a farming method that follows rules about using natural fertilizers and insect control

sustainable (suh-STAYN-uh-buhl): something that can go on for a long time without harming the Earth

Index

Websites

www.epa.gov/kids/

www.meetthegreens.pbskids.org

calc.zerofootprint.net/youth

www.ecokids.ca/pub/kids_home.cfm

www.dnr.state.wi.us/org/caer/ce/eek

About the Author

Barbara Webb lives in Chicago where she tries to keep her carbon footprint small by taking the bus to work and asking her kids to "please take down the recycling." She has written five green science books for kids.